Chicken Fried Steak for the Soul

for man does not live by biscuits alone

ROY ENGLISH

GIBBS·SMITH
PUBLISHER

Salt Lake City

02 03 04 05   5 4 3 2

Copyright © 1999 Roy English

Published by
Gibbs Smith, Publisher
P.O. Box 667
Layton, Utah 84041

Design by Trudi Gershenov Design, New York, New York
Printed and bound in the U.S.A.

Library of Congress Cataloging-in-Publication Data
English, Roy, 1943-
Chicken fried steak for the soul / Roy English.
    p.   cm.
ISBN 0-87905-884-6
I. Title.
PN6162.E523   1999
818 ' .5402—dc21   98-32068   CIP

1

In its mama's eyes,
every sparrow
is an eagle.

2

Life is a game;
those who love
most, win.

**Admit your mistakes
but don't wallow
in them.**

4

Love is jelly
on the biscuit
of life.

5

Folks who expect
to live happily ever
after had best tend
to it daily.

6

**Work hard
to be good,
not perfect.**

7

A cheerful heart makes a tough job easier.

8

**Never work for an
outfit you don't
believe in.**

9

Don't take too much pride in being a good loser.

10

**Loose tongues and
tight boots cause
a lot of pain.**

11

Doing the Lord's work doesn't pay much, but there's a fine retirement plan.

12

**Criticizing another
man's work won't
improve your own.**

13

Forbidden love is a cactus bloom.

14

**Believing in
something makes
it possible,
not easy.**

15

**Wisdom is mostly
learning how to
pace yourself.**

16

**Envy sickens
a body.**

17

A man can earn
contempt in a
heartbeat. Respect
takes time.

18

**Enthusiasm is the
sauce that flavors
our days.**

19

**The lazy call the
skillful "lucky."**

20

Trees that don't bend
break in the wind.

21

Make it your ambition to lead a quiet life and mind your own business.

22

**When in doubt,
pray on it.**

23

**Forget about justice.
Just do what's right.**

24

For a happy
marriage, view
your mate through
a telescope, not a
microscope.

25

**A whistled tune is
soul music.**

26

**Most shortcuts are
dead ends.**

27

**Figure out what
you stand for—and
what you won't.**

28

**Carrying a grudge
makes a strong
man weak.**

29

When you write an
angry letter, use
a pencil.

30

Forget *who's* right;
remember
what's right.

31

Pride can cripple a
healthy man.

32

Sleeping under the
stars humbles a body.

33

**Developing character
or throwing a steer
involves a struggle.**

34

**Roping and good
manners take
practice.**

35

Old friends started out as new acquaintances.

36

Every mama knows
there is greater joy
in loving than in
being loved.

37

**Jesus loves you.
Deal with it.**

38

A wise man is
quick to listen and
slow to speak.

39

Make yourself
useful. If you can't
weave a blanket,
mend a sock.

40

A man who
doesn't stand for
something will fall
for anything.

41

A person must
meet fear to know
courage.

42

**Express yourself
kindly. Being
honest doesn't
mean being cruel.**

43

**Feeling sorry
for yourself is a
lonely ride.**

44

Your ways teach
more than
your words.

45

Forgiving your
enemy doesn't
guarantee he'll
forgive you, but
it's a start.

46

**Hope is the
seed stock of
happiness.**

47

**Living in the past
is dancing with
a dead man.**

48

If any would not
work, neither
should he eat.

49

**Forgive and forget
the best you can.**

50

You can tell a lot
about a man by what
he doesn't have.

51

**Don't argue just
for the hell of it.**

52

Crooked posts
make crooked
fences.

53

Someone who tells
you how honest
he is may be trying
to convince
himself.

54

Don't take the
scenic route unless
you can slow
down and enjoy
the view.

55

**Man does not
live by biscuits
alone.**

56

Telling another
man's secret is
sneaky and
low-down.

57

When life throws
you for a loop,
enjoy the flight,
then get back in
the saddle.

58

**Thank the Lord for
what he gave you,
what he took
away, and all you
have left.**

59

Saying "please" is
not begging, just
good manners.

60

Man should live below his means and above his values.

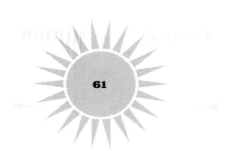

61

**The Good Book is
a comfort on
any trail.**

62

A slow dance with the wrong partner can be a tad awkward. A slow dance with the right partner is one of life's sweetest pleasures.

63

**Don't mistake
kindness for
weakness.**

64

**Learn what's
important and
what's not.**

65

Don't loan money
to a friend. Give it
to him. You'll have
a better chance of
being repaid.

66

**Don't carry tales.
It's not helpful.**

67

It's hard to make
someone smile
without smiling
yourself.

68

In old age, few
regret the risks
they took.

**The bull at
the front of the
herd has the
best view.**

70

There is a shovel
to fit every hand.
Find yours.

71

**Adversity
strengthens a man—
to a point.**

72

A prayer is a kiss
on an angel's
cheek.

73

Don't envy your
sister. The violet
is not diminished
by the beauty
of the rose.

74

A fella who is
wishy on one side
is likely washy on
the other.

75

A steady man
changes without
changing.

76

**What you show a
child, she shows
the world.**

**A guilty heart
convicts itself.**

78

It's easier to lead a
horse with an
apple than to herd
him with a stick.

79

**Cowboys and
Indians are
children of the
same God.**

80

The self-righteous
messenger spoils
the message.

81

Little habits,
good or bad, can
take over a man.

82

Horse races are often
won by a nose—
and a heart.

83

**Everybody is
ignorant about
something.**

84

Little folks have
big ears and even
bigger eyes.

85

**A persuasive man
has more than
one vote.**

86

Don't swat a
gnat with a
baseball bat.

87

**Sour grapes make
bitter wine.**

88

Smiles are free,
frowns are expensive.

89

Learn from the
teapot: whistle
when you need to
let off steam.

90

**Passion
is the ice cream
of summer.
Taste it.**

91

**Thou shalt not
grumble.**

92

A liar is just a lazy thief.

93

**A man who would
die for something
has something
to live for.**

94

You must trust
yourself before you
can trust another.

95

If you would be
loved, try being
lovable.

96

The desires of the diligent are fully satisfied.

— Proverbs 13:4

97

In body language,
a smile is poetry.

98

**Pain is the
sternest teacher.**

99

**Respect is love in
work clothes.**

100

A pennyweight of
doing is worth more
than a pound of
promising.

101

**One determined
woman is a
powerful lot.**

102

Tender hearts can
abide in rugged
places.

103

**A whiny companion
makes for a
hard day.**

104

Life isn't always fair, but things have a way of working out.

105

It takes more than
having kids to
be a daddy.

106

**Humility is the
hardest lesson.**

107

A snorer hears
everyone's snoring
but his own.

108

**A heart knows things
a head never will.**

109

A horse is only as
good as the man in
the saddle.

110

It's hard to get a
handle on a problem
when you're sitting
on your hands.

111

**Experience is a
great teacher if
it doesn't kill
you first.**

112

Wants and needs
are two different
things.

113

Advice is no better
than the one who
gives it.

114

Be careful when choosing heroes.

115

**Keep talking to
your kids,
no matter what.**

116

Cheap boots are rarely a bargain.

117

The truth is simple—hard but simple.

118

Love is medicine—
for the one
who gives it and
for the one
who receives it.

119

**Behold the gift of a
brand new day.**

120

Never cuss when you're with somebody— or when you're alone.

121

You can tell a lot
about a man by how
he shakes hands.

122

**Pray for goodness,
not things.**

123

**Even fools are wise
when silent.**

124

When you have to
make a big decision,
sleep on it.

125

Let another man
praise ye, and not
thine own lips.

Complete your Gibbs Smith, Publisher western humor book library with these other titles by calling toll free: 1·800·748· 5439

Don't Whiz on a 'Lectric Fence

When I Am An Old Coot

Don't Squat With Yer Spurs On!

Don't Squat With Yer Spurs On! II

Never Ask a Man the Size of His Spread

Just One Fool Thing After Another

Laughing Stock

Horse Sense

50 Good Reasons To Be / Not To Be a Cowboy

Cow Chips Aren't for Dippin'